101 Secrets for Lead Generation through Digital Marketing

SAYED N.

DEDICATION

I am dedicating this book to my Parents Altaf Ahmed and Gohar Bano, my loving wife Rabiya and my daughter, Rafiya Sayed.

- Sayed N.

CONTENTS

DIGITAL MARKETING BASIC CERTIFICATION COURSE FOR FREE

To help you to get started in Digital Marketing, I created a FREE bonus Digital Marketing Basic Certification course for you that includes downloadable resources, worksheets, bonus video content.

All the resources that you need to get started with Digital Marketing as a career, consultant or entrepreneur.

So I highly recommend you to enroll to the course right now.

Visit the following link to get free access to your course now –

http://bit.ly/GETDMMC

INTRODUCTION TO DIGITAL MARKETING

Digital Marketing is the process of attracting people/businesses into indicating an interest in your company's products or services using all the digital platforms, be it using Social Media, SEO, Display Ads, Email Marketing, Content Marketing, Video Marketing and Chatbot Marketing.

We need to continuously engage, nurture and convert our target audience with the help of all the available digital marketing platforms and make the cold audience into our loyal customers.

In this book, I will share 101 secrets with you on how you can generate leads or sales for your business through effective Digital Marketing Strategies.

So let's get started.

CONVERSION OPTIMIZATION ON YOUR WEBSITE

1. Homepage Video

If a picture is worth a thousand words, then a video is worth a million. Having a clear 60-second video on your website will help to get uplift in conversions. If possible, have members of your team in the video as people buy from people.

Having your product/service explained by the people who make or deliver it will be invaluable to your target audience. So don't forget to add the video explaining about your products/services and familiarize your company team members and yourself to the target audience because that's the way you can build trust.

2. Website Pop Ups

A study says, a 27% uplift in leads when displaying an attractive and effective popup on the website or a landing page.

Popups are a great way to convert cold website visitors into a lead.

What makes a popup effective is to ensure you offer something of value that someone will want to download in exchange for their contact details, for example, a free report, case study, cheat sheet, e-book or price list. This is what we call an info-swap.

3. Less Is More

The less text that you have on your site, the higher the likelihood is that someone will read it. When you're designing a website home page, don't try to fit everything you have on your website into the one page.

Instead, use succinct copy and large text that is easy to read. Your core message should be simple and speak to the needs of your target audience.

The average visitor doesn't want to comb through an excessive amount of content to understand what your company does. The more concise you are with your messaging, the more effective it will be.

4. A Compelling Call-To-Action

Call-To-Action's like "read more" or "learn more" aren't very compelling and are quite generic. These buttons are how you encourage visitors to engage with your brand online, and if the language you use doesn't capture their interest, they won't click on them.

For example, if you're a travel company and offer New Year Eve Special packages or exclusive promotions on your website, a Call-To-Action that reads "let's go" will be more likely to entice clicks than a Call-To-Action that lacks a unique or intriguing message.

5. Simple Website Forms

Companies that aim to generate leads online should use online forms as a staple. If you're a B2B or a B2C organization, offering a contact form that allows potential customers to enquire, ask a question, or request a quote will be incredibly beneficial if created with the user in mind.

To increase the likelihood of a visitor converting, ask for the bare minimum and make sure the contact form is placed in the most prominent place on a page. Top right through all our tests has proven the best for the website visitors.

6. Don't Forget Mobile Website Visitors

In 2020, 80% of the website visitors will come through mobile devices.

So you cannot neglect mobile visitors. They take a large percentage of your website visitors. Your website should be responsive to provide excellent user experience to your website visitors who are coming to your site from mobile.

The best way to cater for this is to have a responsive website that changes sizes based upon the device a user is browsing your website from. To this end, always think of mobile users when you're in the design process and how everything from text to button size will appear on a screen significantly smaller than a desktop. Make sure that the font is big enough so that users on their smartphone can easily read it, and the call-to-action button is optimized for the size of a thumb instead of a traditional mouse and keyboard that you would have on a desktop.

GENERATING LEADS FROM EMAIL MARKETING

7. Main Message and Call-to-Action Above the Fold

If your main call-to-action falls below the fold, as many as 70% of recipients won't see it. To clarify, above the fold, is the portion of the email that is visible in a reading pane when the email opens.

The portion of the email that requires scrolling to see content is called "below the fold." It may sound obvious, but many people do tend to leave a call-to-action or even the punch line of what they want to say to the very end of an email, by which time it may well be too late. My recommendation is that any call-to-action should be repeated at least three times throughout the email, starting above the fold.

8. Incentives to Increase Email Open Rates

When you include an incentive in your subject line, you can increase open rates by as much as 50%. "Free shipping when you spend $25 or more" or "Receive a free iPhone 11" are examples of good, incentive-focused subject lines.

9. Use Auto-Responders for Opt-Ins

Be prepared for your readers to forget they opted in. Set up an auto-responder that reminds people they opted into your email database. The auto-responder should be sent out one day, five days, and ten days after the person registers. Each auto-responder email should include additional content or bonus material to reward the readers for opting in.

10. Closely Tie Emails to Landing Pages

Your landing page should match the email in terms of headline, copy, and content. The look and feel of your landing page should also match the email. And make sure you're utilizing tracking tools like Google Analytics to see which emails and landing pages performed the best.

GENERATING LEADS FROM YOUTUBE

11. Create Your YouTube Channel

Any business can launch a YouTube channel; you don't have to be a film or entertainment company to do that. A video is a form of content that's continuing to rise in popularity. According to YouTube, about five billion unique users visit YouTube each month.

"Thousands of channels are making six figures a year," YouTube says. Business owners would be foolish not to take advantage of this huge market.

12. YouTube End Cards and Information Buttons

YouTube allows you to add end cards and information buttons to your uploaded videos.

You can take leverage to these features to your benefits. Using end cards, You can give a link back to your website and show the other relevant videos either from your channel or other member s channel to provide more resourceful videos.

And using informational buttons, You can show the polls and provide specific videos for further reference at a particular time duration when the video is playing.

13. Create Informational YouTube Videos

You should create an informative YouTube video rather than transactional or navigational videos. This will give you a competitive advantage to generate high-quality leads.

Informative videos could be "How to" "should be" "Must have" etc. on a specific topic can drive a lot of views from your audience that you are looking to target.

So give your audience a value as much as you can in the form of information in your videos.

14. Brand Your Videos

Make sure people know your videos are part of your company's offerings. At the very least, you should have an intro card at the beginning of your video and a card with your logo at the end. That way, when people run across your videos online, they can associate the content with your company.

Make sure to have your website in your video or video description as well as in your YouTube channel, so that people can locate you online. After all, people have to know who you are before their interest in your videos can translate into sales.

15. Use your YouTube Videos Comments Section

YouTube isn't like advertising on television. Viewers don't usually have the ability to discuss TV ads with the producer; YouTube allows them to participate in the conversation in real-time.

Make it easy for them by enabling comments and responding to them right away. You can also devote future videos to popular comments. If your viewers feel their voice is being heard, they will become your loyal to your YouTube channel, and you will be able to grow your subscribers base.

16. YouTube Analytics

YouTube analytics provides you with a very detailed report on every aspect of your channel views.

Like from which sources they have come from, how much minutes/seconds they have viewed your video, their demographics and interests etc.

All these insights you can analyse from YouTube analytics and translate these reports to improvise and grow your channel further.

17. Partner with YouTube Influencers

Sometimes life is a little easier when you leverage someone else's audience, so instead of slogging away building an audience and converting everybody all on your own, find out who the most influential YouTube channels are in your field. Approach these people about creating a collaborative video on a topic of mutual interest.

Make your topic as interactive as possible to raise interest. If you succeed, you'll have the benefit of accessing a much larger audience. Your credibility will also rise as a result of partnering with an expert, which will help increase your conversion rates.

GENERATING LEADS FROM LINKEDIN

18. Perfect Your LinkedIn Bio

Prepare a written version of your 30-Second elevator pitch and include that text in your LinkedIn profile. The main thing to remember about LinkedIn is that it's a huge, never-ending, virtual networking event, and you have to be ready with the right response to, "What do you do?"

Your profile bio is the answer to that question, as told from a prospect in pain that eventually turned into your happy customer.

19. Add a Video to Your LinkedIn Profile

LinkedIn provides the ability to add videos to both your bio and the write-ups on each of your current roles.

It gives you lots of opportunities to gain views on YouTube videos which you link to your profile, and to implement calls-to-actions within the videos to draw prospects off LinkedIn and into marketing funnels on your website.

20. Add More Connections to your LinkedIn Network

LinkedIn works in a tiered fashion with three tiers. When you connect with someone, you are a 1st-degree connection; their 1st-degree connections become your 2nd-degree connections, and so on.

Don't be over-selective about who you pick to be connected with. You don't have to be friends with them; this is a network building tool and a great one for prospecting. If you invest a minute or so each working day clicking the "connect" button on the "People, You May Know" list that LinkedIn posts in your feed you will broaden your network and with it the potential of more leads.

21. Connect you Mail App to LinkedIn

Look for plugins to Microsoft Outlook to connect with people that you email directly within Microsoft Outlook. Mac's and almost all other mail clients also have a plugin; this means that you never miss a chance to connect with prospects at the right moment, which is usually when you are at the forefront of their mind, i.e. immediately after they have emailed you.

22. Follow Client's and Prospect's LinkedIn Company Pages

Look up your current clients and top prospects and find out whether they have a company page. If they do, follow and monitor it. Comment on their posts and if appropriate, write recommendations for them.

You can also see who else works at that company and connect with as many of them as you feel necessary and start the conversation with them by offering them a value in the form of information related to your niche.

23. Post a Daily LinkedIn Update

Spend 60 seconds each working day posting an "Update" to your LinkedIn network. Use the daily update to share a link to an article or a video that is relevant to your prospects and customers.

Each time you post an update you get displayed on the feed of all the people with whom you are connected. But never sell when you post updates! Add value and share expertise instead, which will help you to build the trust factor among your target audience and later you can harvest that trust into a hot lead waiting to award you a sale/contract.

24. Join LinkedIn Groups

LinkedIn lets you connect with people who are in groups with you; this is an excellent way of linking to others who are not 2nd level contacts. It also allows you to network and talks to likeminded users. Make sure when operating within these groups that you add value to others, share insights, and build out your network with prospects.

25. Use LinkedIn to Celebrate the Accomplishments of Others

When you come across a news story or post that offers good news about your client or prospect, or any key contact, share the news as a status update. Recognize the person with an "@" reply. That will ensure they receive notification of the mention. It is a great way to share the love, but also stay on their radar in a positive 'non-salesy' way.

26. Write LinkedIn Recommendations

It is often challenging to secure LinkedIn recommendations, if only because it takes the writer time to log in, write, and post them. Instead of waiting for someone to recommend you, devote five minutes a day to writing and posting (reality-based) recommendations for your customers and key contacts. Once your connection approves the text, the recommendation will show up on his/her LinkedIn account. This will align you with your contact, serve as a permanent top-of-mind promotional piece for you and your organization, show your network that you work together, and make it far more likely that your contact will look for a way return the favour. That could be either a referral or a recommendation.

27. Download your Connections and Market to them

LinkedIn allows you to do a full excel database download of all of your connection's details and email addresses. This creates so many opportunities to do email marketing to them. You could also target them on Facebook or using LinkedIn Ads by uploading them as a custom audience to the ads platform network.

GENERATING LEADS FROM FACEBOOK

28. Setup a Facebook business page

Facebook is a powerhouse of conversation, and with over 2.45 billion users by the end of 2019 and no signs of this slowing down, your customers are becoming more likely than unlikely to be on Facebook. It creates a strong case for having an engaging and continually updated facebook business page. You can share your news, thoughts and links to other content, best still you can engage directly as your business with potential clients. If you are not on Facebook as your business, you will be missing out.

29. Share links to content on your Facebook Page's feed

Once you are set up, you now need to ensure that you are allowing your Facebook followers to convert into leads. The simplest way to do this is to take the same content that you're using to generate leads on your website and share links to that content on your Facebook Page's feed. It works particularly well if the link directs people to a landing page with a lead generation form for downloadable content such as an eBook or a webinar/cheatsheet. Links to blog content can be shared as well, but be sure each blog post you share also has a call-to-action to a relevant landing page with a conversion form so that visitors can ultimately convert. Blog content isn't as streamlined for lead generation as direct links to landing pages are, but blog posts can help initiate lead generation too.

30. Using the Facebook Business Page to GO LIVE and Stories

Facebook LIVE is the excellent feature for businesses; You can organize LIVE workshops, product or services launch, interact with your followers and hold Q&A sessions and everything in between you can think of to increase the engagement on your company Facebook page. You should use the Facebook LIVE at least every week to interact with your followers; this builds the commitment and trust among your audience.

You should also be using Facebook stories feature to let your followers know the latest happening which is going on in your company. Share your teammate's photo, which assignment you are working on or some fun activities.

31. Add the Facebook Like plugin & share buttons to content

You should make it easy for others who are consuming your web content and allow them to share that content in their Facebook feed so it would be easier for you to spread the word about your business products or service.

Add the Facebook Like plugin and 'Share on Facebook' button to every piece of content that you produce upon your blog, to give an extra boost of reach when someone wants to share or like it.

32. Using the Facebook Pixel

Facebook pixels is a Javascript code which you need to place on your website with the help of your web developer.

Pixel code is used to drop a cookie that will track visitors on your website so that you can advertise to them later with highly personalized ads. This means if someone has been on your website, you can follow them back to Facebook and Instagram with an offer which they can't refuse like exclusive discounts, cheatsheet download, strategy sheet or some useful information for your target audience.

33. Facebook Ads

With Facebook Ads, You can promote any size of businesses and increase brand awareness, generate leads and make sales for your products or services.

You can run ads throughout the customer journey of your target audience right from the awareness stage to consideration and then purchase.

You will be allowed to laser target your audience based on the country, age group, sex, interests/behaviours and many other advanced sets of targetting options to connect with your audience and show them the ads in the feed.

Facebook Ads includes different type of campaigns like Leads ads, Dynamic ads, Page engagement ads, catalogue sales ads, traffic ads, conversion ads, messenger ads and many others.

The ads contain both image and interactive video ads.

34. Facebook Custom Audiences

It is a killer Facebook Ads strategy which you must use when running the Facebook Ads for your business.

Using custom audiences, you can build the different sets of audiences of your website visitors, page followers, people who are interacting with your ads, upload your email database from CRM etc.

You can also build lookalike audiences to target those people who are very similar to your core custom audiences to expand the reach of your advertising campaign.

GENERATING LEADS FROM TWITTER

35. Twitter

Twitter, when used effectively, can be great for generating leads. If you need convincing to set up your account and to use it regularly, success comes to those who use the platform actively to reach out to influencers in their industry and get into conversations with them. Their followers, who are likely some of your potential customers, will see your interactions and follow you or visit your site. You can also follow trending hashtags that pertain to your business and interject your thoughts into the general discussion by using the # symbol. For instance, if you are in the mobile phone world, you may use #iphone11 to find and eventually get leads.

36. Search Keywords and Hashtags on Twitter

Twitter has over 400 million users around the world, so it's a good bet that most of your target audience is on the platform. Are you taking advantage of that by actively looking for and talking with them? If not, start by making a list of keywords and hashtags related to your business name, your product names and even your competitors and their products. Use that list to conduct a simple search on Twitter. Browse through the search results to find and follow prospects that you think are interested in your business and products. Engage with them by retweeting their content and using @mentions to connect personally.

37. Pay Attention to Off-Topic Tweets

People regularly tweet to express their likes, motivations, lifestyles, desires and aspirations. It makes it easy for you to tap into these insights without formal (and costly) market research. Don't just use the apparent product or service related hashtags, make a note of any other topics that your prospects tweet about. This way, you can get to know what your consumers' interests are outside of your offerings. You might find, for example, a trend in the hashtags that your followers use, specific lifestyle preferences or common life goals. The better you understand your market's demographics, the more effectively you can market and sell to them.

38. Host Twitter Polls

Organizing contests provide more than attention and engagement. You can gain consumer insight, increase your email leads, learn about product preferences and more. To get the best leads, offer a prize with value directly related to your business. That way, you'll incentivize people to participate, but more importantly, you'll attract people who are genuinely interested in what your business has to offer.

39. Tweet Quotes, Questions and Trivia

Quotes, questions and trivia are some of the most shared content on Twitter. Quotes can inspire and create a 'me too' feeling that results in retweets and click-throughs. The quotes you tweet don't have to be from famous people; try using your content. Highlight witty quotes from your latest eBook or another product.

40. Tweet Likes and Retweets (RTs)

Questions provoke engagement by understanding consumers interest in your content. Tweet out the questions you get asked most and let people know that they can find the answers on your website (don't forget to include a link to the exact page). Asking the right questions gets you the most retweets and likes.

41. Use Twitter Cards

Twitter cards take tweets beyond 140 characters; they let you add images, videos and product descriptions. To use them, you must have an advertising account with Twitter. While there are eight different kinds of Twitter cards, the product and lead generation cards are the best for lead generation. Twitter product cards give you up to 200 characters for product descriptions. You can include your product's title, description and a small image, as well as sales-friendly information such as availability, price and location. Twitter lead generation cards are an easy way to collect email leads. When someone clicks on the card, it auto-populates with the email address associated with that user's Twitter account. Twitter lead generation cards work best when you give your followers an offer they can't refuse, like a giveaway or contest entry, coupons or free trials.

GENERATING LEADS FROM INSTAGRAM

42. Create either Creator or Business Instagram Account

You shouldn't be using Personal Instagram account ever; Always switch Instagram account to either creator or business account.

You will unlock additional features of Instagram like insights, email, website, phone number and then a business category, which will be visible in your Instagram profile.

43. Instagram Hashtags Strategy

Apart from your image, your hashtags are the most crucial element of your post. While captions help you tell the story behind your image, hashtags allow you to get your image (and caption) seen by those outside your current sphere of followers. When users search for relevant industry-related hashtags, you want your posts to show up. There are three main strategies you can use for choosing hashtags: 1. Use popular hashtags that have the best chance of getting searched for (e.g., #iphone11, #ipad, etc.) 2. Use less popular hashtags yet highly-relevant hashtags. These may drive fewer users to your posts, but the ones who do find you will be more targeted. 3. Use hashtags commonly thought to attract new followers. Some of the most widely used are #followme, #follow4follow and #follow. Whichever strategy you use, try to use at least one hashtag on each post. Don't worry about using too many hashtags; some research even suggests that engagement is highest on posts that have 11+ hashtags!

44. Use Instagram Stories and IGTV feature frequently

Instagram stories and IGTV are a great way to connect with your followers on Instagram.

Almost 90% of the users check their Instagram stories, so don't miss out to feature your products and services on Instagram stories.

Use this feature to show around your office, testimonials of your team members, latest happening, new projects that you have been working on etc.

IGTV is another great feature which you can use it for your business to upload videos of up to 60 minutes in vertical video format.

45. Show off Your Product / Service

Because Instagram feels far more like beautiful people sharing beautiful photos and videos, brands forget to show off their actual products and services. After all, the whole reason you're using Instagram in the first place is to get potential customers to become paying customers. You'd be doing yourself a great disservice if you didn't leverage Instagram as a platform for showcasing products to your followers in the best possible visual format as you can to tell your brand story.

46. Plan collaboration with Instagram influencers

The idea of collaboration with Instagram Influencers has already been gaining traction for brands looking at a better return for money invested in marketing. The term describes Instagram users who typically have around 10,000 to 200,000 followers. The Influencers have made it but are not up in the heavens with the millions of followers, and so when they share content for a brand it is still secondary to their fulltime profession; they post sponsored content less often than more prominent social celebrities, and so the posts feel more authentic. With the same amount of budget, brands can collaborate with 20 or 40 influencers to reach different demographics and see better engagement, compared to one or two celebrities.

GENERATING LEADS FROM TIKTOK

47. Connect with Millennials

TikTok should be part of your overall content promotion strategy, as you could connect well with the young target audience aged between 13 - 35 as a millennials target audience.

You can post vertical videos about your products and services and other entertaining content that resonates well with your products and services so you will be able to build the audience on TikTok better.

48. Show Your Product or Service in Action

Make it a habit to show your product or service in action. This non-salesy "show not tell" method works great for both product-based businesses and service-based businesses. If you run a service-based business, you should talk about what you're up to each day, what you're working on, and even shine a light on your clients and let them speak to your TikTok followers. For product-based businesses, show your product being used, a behind-the-scenes look at how it's made, and different uses for your product. The key to success is letting your TikTok followers know how to take the first step in buying your product or service and making it easy for them.

49. Run TikTok Ads

TikTok Ads are a great way to reach out to your potential audience on the TikTok app.

You can run brand awareness, traffic and conversions as campaigns to send people back to your website to take a specific action like case study download, strategy sheet or even webinar registrations etc.

50. Qualify Warm Prospects with a TikTok Giveaway

Giveaways are a great way to generate and build an email list, but they don't necessarily equate to leads. So instead of doing a giveaway for something like an iPhone 11, offer giveaways that are qualifying and that have some intent. For example, an ice cream parlour might do a giveaway for a free scoop of ice cream every day for a week as the main prize.

People who enter the competition have qualified themselves as being in the area and the market for your ice cream. If you collect details and ask to keep in touch in some way during your giveaway, you can classify these entrants as potential leads and future customers whom you can now contact.

So the first step is to decide what you can give away that will generate qualified leads for your business. Once you have the idea, announce it to your TikTok audience via your story. Perhaps announce it a few times during the week or make a big deal of it leading up to the giveaway at the end of the week.

The good thing about Tiktok is that after 24 hours the story (and thus the competition) are gone, so there's a sense of urgency for people to enter the contest on impulse.

GENERATING LEADS FROM CONTENT MARKETING

51. Blog

Having a blog is one of the best lead generating tools you can use, as it not only allows a company (or person) complete control of what is said but also an opportunity to have the undivided attention of the reader. Make sure that your blog is optimized to generate leads by having a sign-up newsletter section for your lead magnet and by using the contact details of the lead to promote your products and services.

52. Guest Blogging

Guest blogging is a process of posting articles on other people's or company's blogs. It's an opportunity to take your expertise and share it with others, as well as a chance to increase traffic to both parties' blogs. Guest blogging is also a great way to establish yourself as an authority figure within your industry niche and build relationships with other bloggers and experts within your field. The ultimate goal is to draw the other blogs traffic back to your website so you can convert them into a lead, so make sure you add call-to-actions on your blog pages.

53. Allow other bloggers to guest post on your blog

Since guest blogging should be a two-way street, you should also consider featuring posts developed by guest bloggers. Featuring guest posts will also expose your audience to a new perspective and fresh new content. We are all guilty of falling victim to a routine and getting tired of the same old stuff, so this will keep them engaged and coming back for more. It also adds content to your website, which will help your SEO, plus they may also promote it to their audience, and you may gain new audiences for your business from there.

54. Comment on other blogs

Look for blogs with industry-related information and post some comments. Make sure you comment something exciting and in par with the tone of other comments. Your fellow 'commenters' will get to know you and will start to follow links that you post and then start to read content on your website or start to download lead magnets that you have set up on your blog pages.

55. eBooks

As you are reading this, you are a great example that eBooks work great for B2B companies or a business that works in a very technical space, as people love to read and gain expertise about their industry. Make sure you don't promote your services or products. People don't want to be sold; they want to be informed. So write it from a neutral perspective and give actionable insights.

56. Monthly Email Newsletter

An email newsletter is an online version of an old-school newsletter. It is one of the simplest ways to generate a subscriber base, but going forward you will need to be punchy as many people will always ask 'what is in it for me?' before subscribing.

Once you know why you are writing one and for who, make sure you put a newsletter sign up in every possible place that makes sense on your website and give them a strong reason why they should subscribe to your Email Newsletter in the exchange of sharing their contact information.

57. Infographics

Infographics may have been overused a few years back, but people still share them and always stop and read them whenever they can. There are loads of free tools so they can be relatively cheap to produce. Come up with an original idea, interesting statistics, a case study or thought leadership based concepts and make it into a graphic representation of the point you would like to deliver. Then share with as many people as possible. Always put your business logo and website URL on the bottom of the infographic.

This way, readers will be able to visit your site. Don't forget that there are infographic specific websites that you can share too, plus image leads social networks like Facebook, Instagram or Pinterest are great places to start.

58. Write Whitepapers

A whitepaper typically goes deeper into the subject matter than a product or datasheet. Whitepapers are more solution-oriented and academic. Provide your whitepapers when someone fills out a form for higher business to business lead generation results from your website. Studies have shown that white papers are highly viral; that is, they are passed around by 60% of technology professionals according to a study by MarketingSherpa and KnowledgeStorm. White papers are considered to be credible resources for thought leadership and subject matter expertise.

59. Create a bundled kit around your subject matter

Don't limit your content to just a whitepaper. Bundle various types of material such as a whitepaper, slide deck, and recorded webinar, checklist, strategy sheet into a bundled kit. This makes your content more valuable than your competitors and saves your prospects time in hunting for each of these types of content individually.

60. Create a comparison or review guide

Create a guide that compares your product to others in the industry. When a lead discovers your product early in the buying process, it might appear to them that your product is the same or even better as your competitors. A comparison guide will differentiate your product and clarify any misperception.

61. Have a Survey Running on your Website

It is an excellent excuse to have a touchpoint with your prospects and to get them thinking when on your website. The best way to do this is to have a simple one-question survey, with several answers displayed so they can just quickly answer. The best survey widgets will show the results live on your website. You can then blog about the results, and this additional linger time on your site might get your prospect to convert.

GENERATING LEADS FROM GOOGLE

62. Organic SEO

Organic Search Engine Optimization (SEO) is when you try to rank for select keywords without paying for ads to appear in the sponsored sections.

SEO is ideal for generating leads, mainly through organic google searches that consumers use every day. Good ranking in search results means higher visibility for your website, which in turn should create a steady flow of enquiries for your related products/services.

There are two main areas you will need to get right to achieve results from SEO. Firstly you need to make sure all your on-page content and Metadata is focused around the keywords you want to rank for. The second is to get as many links from other websites back to your website as this shows popularity.

The better the authority of the site that links to you, the better the link in Google search engine eyes.

63. Link Building

When other sites link to your website, it's like getting a vote. The more votes you have, the more popularity or authority, the search engines believe you have. Link building is a core strategy to get listed on the front page of google search. Focus on both the quality and quantity of your links. One hack is to go out to your network and ask them to give you a link; if you know them well, you can usually get a few useful links quickly.

64. Google Ads Pay-Per-Click (PPC)

Although expensive, PPC can pay dividends. Make sure you budget appropriately and use keywords with low competition that are relevant to your business. While your competitors are paying 10X what you might per click, you could be grabbing some low-cost leads. However, it is essential to understand with PPC that you need to be prepared to jump in feet first. Many small business owners try to "dip their toe in the water," and spend a couple of hundred dollars to see what happens.

In most cases, that strategy ends up being a complete waste of money. Google Ads is a game of numbers, and unless you're lucky, the math won't work out on your

$200 tester budget. If you're not drawing enough traffic that a 2-4% conversion rate on your landing/offer page won't be meaningful, your Google Ads spending is almost guaranteed to be wasted. If you want to try this, be prepared to go all-in for a couple of months at least, it's the only way you'll get any real idea of what your campaign is capable of.

65. Use a Dedicated PPC landing page

Imagine walking into a car dealership knowing the exact model and colour of the vehicle you want to buy. But when you ask to see one, the salesman instead gives you a full tour of the showroom, explaining the features and benefits of all their cars. You'd be annoyed and would probably buy your car elsewhere. That's how your visitors will feel if they click on your Google Ads link and end up on your home page. They are looking for information on something particular, and your ad told them that you might be a good fit. So why waste their time? Create a landing page that explains exactly why your business/products/services are a good match for them and provide a CLEAR call to action (CTA) for next steps.

66. Improve your Google Ads Quality Score

If you're trying to master PPC, you need a solid understanding of Quality Score. Your Quality Score has a significant influence on the cost and effectiveness of your PPC campaigns. Quality Score is Google's rating of the quality and relevance of both your keywords and PPC ads.

It is used to determine your cost per click (CPC) and multiplied by your maximum bid to determine your ad rank in the ad auction process. Once improved, you will be given higher ad rankings and lower costs per click.

67. Google Ads various campaign types

Whichever kind of business you may be running, Googe Ads can fit into all size of business and all types of business.

You can select from a wide range of campaign types which are available in the Google Ads interface.

If your business is looking to generate brand recall value, then you may run a brand awareness campaign. If your business objective is to get more leads and sales, then you can lead ads or conversion ads to be specific.

YouTube ads are also available from the Google Ads interface itself so you can set up even YouTube various ad formats as well to connect with your target audience and increase your business leads and sales.

68. Google My Business

Google My Business is a free marketing tool that connects customers with businesses. It is what drives the pins for each business on Google Maps. Once you create your account, you will benefit from appearing for Local Searches.

Google says 70 per cent of mobile consumers that search for local business visits it within a day of the search, and 25 per cent of consumers make a purchase. The other benefit is that all of the information you list is clickable.

Customers can click your phone number to call on their smartphones or tap your website address to see your site. You can also post pictures and videos to your page. You can also ask your customers to add reviews so that you start to appear at the top of search results as an authoritative business in your niche.

OFTEN OVERLOOKED ONLINE LEAD GENERATION METHODS

69. Online Chat

Often people leave your website because they never really belonged there. Your product or service just wasn't a good fit, and that's OK. But sometimes visitors leave for the WRONG reasons: a minor misunderstanding about what your product does, a feature that isn't explicitly listed, a particular question that your web copy didn't overtly answer. Often, these visitors won't take the time to call, nor will they fill out your email form and wait for a response. But many will engage in a live online chat with an operator who can help answer their questions. It has been reported that it's not uncommon for a conversation to boost conversion rates by 15-25% or more.

70. Start a Podcast

Podcasts are everywhere now and accessible through Google Podcasts, Apple iTunes, the internet, iPhone's, iPads and more. Podcasts are great for business travellers who download podcasts and listen to it while on the road. It's sort of like a magazine subscription but in an audio format. When people subscribe, they'll get the latest podcasts to catch up on. Getting your solutions out through this channel is innovative and puts your message in more hands.

71. Webinars

Webinars are an inexpensive way to get your message to thousands of potential customers. Many services allow you to broadcast a webinar quickly and easily. And if you make it a recurring event, you'll continue to grow your following. So, come up with a great idea that helps your customers and promote it using social media, your network and your newsletter. At the end of the webinar, feel free to ask the attendees to download an eBook, sign up for your newsletter, or visit your site. It will bring the leads flowing in.

72. Join industry forums

Research the industry forums in your business niche and get involved wherever you can. There are always buoyant conversations happening if you find the right forum and like direct mail, with the emergence of social media, you find forums are getting less spam. Therefore real conversations are more natural to have with likeminded users.

OLD SCHOOL MARKETING THAT STILL WORKS IN TODAY'S DIGITAL WORLD 2020 AND BEYOND

73. Publish a book

Writing a book takes time but pays big dividends, trust me! It has been the catalyst for gaining more prospects, or speaking gigs and ultimately helped to propel you into The Apprentice TV show.

74. Get Media Coverage

Do you know what journalists hate? Being hit up by dozens of PR agencies hour after hour, day after day. Do you know what journalists hate a little less? Having an owner of a company reach out to them and tell their story in a real and authentic manner. Your chances of being covered go up significantly if you do the reach out yourself (as long as your pitch is on point). A few tips regarding reaching out to journalists: Don't mass email them do not open with "to whom it may concern" and don't annoy them (one follow up email is sufficient). By getting your name out in the media, you begin to develop a following, increase your brand and come off as an expert in your domain – all that can help you get leads.

75. Strong Branding

Customers love trustworthy companies. They like it when a company has a loud and clear message, and that message is consistent across all of their marketing platforms. So, don't try and be everything to everyone. Customers want the experts and the company that is the best in their industry. Focus on communicating that through your branding and your conversion rates will go up, resulting in more leads.

76. Outsource your cold calling

Cold calling is not everyone's favourite thing to do and is usually last on the list for salespeople, but there are firms out there that do nothing but business to business lead generation and demand generation for you. Some firms get paid only when they generate a "qualified" lead, others get paid when they generate a meeting, and some get paid a fixed income based on a set of goals. The good news is that contracts with these companies are typically short term. Try it out; if it doesn't work, you can always walk away.

77. Direct Mail

Email marketing has replaced direct mail strategies for many companies, and it's somewhat of a dying approach. It could be an opportunity for you to do something that others don't. However, direct mail can be expensive. Identify what other companies are already doing in your targeted area first. The key to direct mail is differentiation. Make your content stand out and irritable to the recipient.

78. Send Cards on Public Holidays

One of the ways my grandfather grew his textile business was to send cards to his customers on exciting public holidays. For example, he'd send Independence Day cards and Happy New Year greetings with personalize messages to his customers; none of his competitors did so, and therefore the competition on the doorstep was not cluttered. His response rate was excellent, and yours will be too as the door is entirely uncluttered in modern days, as well as gift cards becoming a dying practice. It will differentiate you and give you that all-important attention.

79. Sponsor a charity event

Charity events can be an excellent way of getting many of your hottest prospects to a dinner or a networking event without it feeling like you are trying to sell to them. Most Charities have gala dinners where you can sponsor a table of 10 and bring all your hottest clients and prospects too. Plus the feel-good element creates a great story which can be blogged about or even get you into the local newspaper.

80. Sponsor a Local Sports Team

Working with local clubs and local people to help them get a new kit or to refurbish their changing rooms or to sponsor the matchday program is a great way to get your name out there is a feel-good way. Make sure you go to several games and network with people at the club, you never know who might be playing or supporting that team - it could be your perfect prospect.

81. Publicize landmark numbers of new client in the year

It is an exciting hack to create news and get interested. If you make a big deal about getting you 100th client in the year, or your 1,000th or if you are like a small business and do not take 100's of the client a year you could even celebrate 100th client since you set up the business. Whatever you choose, it is all about showing the audience that 100's of businesses have chosen and trusted you. If you do a press release, you may even get a few column inches or a local radio interview.

82. Have a great business card

Most people forget that when they meet other businesses, the one thing that they will take home with them is your business card. If you add a call to action upon it, maybe even a link to downloadable content, you will be able to see when this prospect is active on your website and therefore start to target them with a phone call or other marketing techniques.

83. Your Email Signature

It is prime real estate for marketing, it is at the bottom of every email you send and if you are anything like me you send a lot of emails per day! Add in links to events you are hosting or eBooks they can download, and also include your headshot photo as well in your email signature. It will generate a far better uplift in leads than just your website address.

EVENT MARKETING

84. Exhibitions and Trade Shows

Some wildly successful businesses employ only one primary method of marketing: they display and sell their wares at trade shows, exhibitions, and fairs. They realize that many serious prospects will attend these gatherings. But there is an art to successful exhibiting which, if mastered, generates immense rewards. There are few other sales forums where prospects and clients come to you and where you can meet so many of them in a single day. You can also conduct valuable research, get first hand opinions on your products and services and even collect relevant testimonials. Besides attracting new business, exhibitions can be used to introduce existing customers to additional products and services they were previously unaware of.

85. Attend tradeshows but only walk the floor

Most tradeshows cost thousands of pounds to attend. Shows often require a team to travel, set up equipment and more. Marketing may not have the time or the budget for tradeshows. Instead, send a salesperson or a company executive to "walk the floor". Map out a plan of the companies you want to visit while at the show. When you approach, their booth makes sure first to act very interested in what they're offering and ask questions about their solution. The conversation will naturally shift over as your contact says "so what does your company do?" End the discussion by finding out who the best contact is to share your solution with. Walking the floor vs setting up a booth is a simple, cost-effective way to yield a positive ROI at tradeshows.

86. Sponsor an award

Connect your name with an award to boost brand/name recognition. The award could be a "best in class", "best of breed", "most improved" or an "industry leader in..." award. Get creative; the key is to sponsor the award frequently, so your prospects make a psychological connection between the award and your company. It keeps you top-of-mind with your prospects, crucial for effective lead generation.

87. Speak at Events

The top brass within your business, such as the CEO or CMO (might be you), carry a lot of weight with their title. Look to get a speaking or event schedule in place every year and start talking at events where your prospects can sit in the audience and get to know you on mass.

88. Join a Business Networking Group

My partner and I are members of many networking organisations, two of the most regularly attended are BNI and TiE who offers weekly breakfast meetings and monthly meetups for two hours to meet and get to know other businesses locally.

89. Join a Chamber of Commerce

Again, like business networking, this is a great way to meet many fellow businesses, the chamber also can help with matchmaking if you want to meet specific people in specific industries.

90. Ask your clients what events they go to

No one knows your target market better than your customers do. As a business, you may have four, five, six or more industries you're selling too. Alternatively, your customers live and breathe one industry all the time. Ask them what industry shows they attend, which ones are the best to go to and which ones they'd recommend your company go to. If you end up going, make sure to meet your customer at the show for coffee!

RECOMMENDATIONS, REFERRALS AND TESTIMONIALS

91. Customer Video Testimonials

Testimonials are not usually the first thing people think of when they approach video marketing. They take time and money to make, but if done correctly, you can capture genuine feedback and recommendations from your happy clients. You will find that this type of 'social proof' will be unviable for your marketing, both for lead generation, but also to help get prospects over and objections they may have when they are in your buying funnels.

92. Written Testimonials

Having written testimonials on your website, a Google local listing or any other online directory is an excellent way of getting feedback from your customers. Think about even asking customers to handwrite out a testimonial and the share this as an image on social media, particularly the image lead platforms such as Instagram or Pinterest or even Facebook.

93. Referral Systems

One third-party endorsement is more powerful than a hundred presentations. Getting your customers to recommend and encourage other people they associate with to seek out your products or services is the most coveted prize in selling, besides a sale. There are hundreds of referral systems you can use; to create an unlimited supply of hot prospects; to get prospects returning your calls; to contact hard-to-reach buyers; to create a reputation that opens closed doors; to enhance customer loyalty, and to increase sales and multiply profits. Referral systems make your life easier and more professional, and bring higher profits with increased customer loyalty.

94. Old Clients

Many salespeople tend to think about making new business sales. Many organizations forget to reconnect with past clients, when in fact they may well be the most comfortable people to sell to as they already know, like and trust you.

95. Your Customer's Competitors

Use a Google search or even ask them to find out who your customer's competitors are and then contact them to see if they would like your help. If your customer found value in your solution, their competitors probably will too.

96. Do Lunch

Everyone has to eat! So why not take your customers and prospects out to lunch as much as you can (assuming it fits within your budget). They'll feel relaxed and open up to you. Ask them if they know other companies that could use your solution, ask what the best way is to find additional opportunity within their company or if they know someone else who might like to benefit from what you offer.

ADVANCED DIGITAL MARKETING LEAD GENERATION IDEAS

97. Chatbot marketing

Chatbot marketing is the next big thing in the Digital Marketing space, As it will give you the highest ROI.

You can use the Facebook Messenger chatbots to install it in your website, landing pages and provide them FREE information, and instead of emailing to customers, Send that information via MEssenger chatbots. It will allow you to interact with your customers/prospects right in the Messenger itself one-on-one.

You can also schedule sequences, broadcasts, tag them for the specific series of conversions as you do with the email marketing software.

It is the new generation marketing technique which you should implement in your business as soon as possible.

98. Advanced SEO using Schema Markup

It is the new strategy to get your website rank higher in search using schema markup. You can show the rich results in Google search compare to other websites.

You can show specific information from your website like, photo, video, Frequently Asked questions, reviews, site links etc. to provide users with more information on the search engine itself. It helps in two ways, Increase your Click-Through Rates (CTR's) and lift your ranking higher in search engine.

99. Marketing Automation using Zapier

Zapier is the industry-leading marketing automation tool, which you can use to automate your business marketing.

You don't need to hire a team for all the mundane tasks; It will be taken care of by zapier automated marketing automation between two or multiple apps which you use on a day to day basis.

E.g., Once someone comes to your website and fills a contact form, Then automated system using zapier automatically fill the lead details in Google Sheet and automatically you can put them into your CRM as well. From CRM, you can show them the highly personalized ads through Facebook Ads, and so on.

There are a lot of marketing applications which are cloud-based which we use daily to run our business, but those apps are not connected, and we had to assign someone to copy and paste from one app to another.

Zapier takes cares of all these processes efficiently.

100. Launch Online Course

It would be best if you consider launching an online course to educate the industry fraternity that you are in. In this way, You will be able to establish the authority in your niche as a thought leader.

So plan an online course which you can offer to your niche and sell it for a premium price so others can learn from you and you will be able to lead by the example.

101. Video Creator for your Textual Content

According to the study, 75% of the internet content will be consumed in the video format by 2020.

So it's the right time that you need to invest heavily in videos. You can use the tools like Invideo or Typito to create awesome videos for your blogs/articles and put them along with your textual contents on your website.

It will boost decrease your bounce rate and improve customer interaction on your website and eventually it will lead to more high-quality leads.

CONCLUSION

I hope you learned tons of insights from my book.

I hope it must be resourceful and you are going to implement in your business.

It is a testament to the fact that there are so many ways to generate leads for your business. However, all of it is pointless if you do not implement them, test them and jump in with both feet. Rome was not built in a day, but it was started, persevered with and finally got built. Yet, even Rome needs continuous tweaks, improvements and new things added to it, just like any good marketing campaign. Keep on adding and growing, and you will have multiple lead generating assets that you can be proud of.

All the secrets mentioned in this book may not be appropriate or viable to your specific business marketing needs. You always need to understand your target audience and based on that define the strategy where you need to invest your effort continuously.

I wish you the best in your business marketing.

Best Regards,

Sayed N.

ABOUT THE AUTHOR

A renowned Digital Marketing Strategist, Digital Marketing Consultant, Speaker and Digital Marketing coach with over ten years of progressive experience.

He has been a trusted advisor to businesses from the SMB level up to large enterprises and Fortune 500 companies. He played a pivotal role in the growth and advancement of InnoMind Technologies as the diversified business group which dealt with Digital Marketing training arm, Digital Marketing Franchise arm and full-service Digital Marketing consulting agency serving clients across the globe.

He has an MBA in Marketing & Sales from MDS University and Certified Google Ads partner. He also works closely with various women empowerment agencies globally to promote rural women entrepreneurship and enable them to take their business digital.

Twitter - @noorulsayed

www.ingramcontent.com/pod-product-compliance
Lightning Source LLC
Chambersburg PA
CBHW051205170526
45158CB00005B/1820